To the Fire Station

Written by Lisa Harkrader
Illustrated by Dana Regan
Cover illustrated by Louise Gardner

Louis Weber, C.E.O., Publications International, Ltd.
7373 North Cicero Avenue, Lincolnwood, Illinois 60712

Ground Floor, 59 Gloucester Place, London W1U 8JJ

Customer Service: 1-800-595-8484 or customer_service@pilbooks.com

www.pilbooks.com

Permission is never granted for commercial purposes.

p i kids is a registered trademark of Publications International, Ltd.

ISBN-13: 978-1-4127-9177-9
ISBN-10: 1-4127-9177-4

8 7 6 5 4 3 2 1

publications international, ltd.

My name is Kate, and I'm a firefighter. My job is to put out fires and rescue people who are in trouble.

During my shifts, I live at the fire station. Firefighters work 24-hour shifts and take turns staying at the fire station.

When the alarm sounds, we are always available and can go quickly to a fire or to an accident.

On the first floor of our fire station, there are big garages. This is where we keep all of the fire engines.

One kind of fire engine is called a ladder truck. It has a long ladder that can reach the top floors of tall buildings. We use the ladder to rescue people and pets who can't get out of the building by themselves.

Another kind of fire engine is called a pumper truck. It pumps water from a fire hydrant through a long, thick hose.

The tanker truck carries a huge tank of water. The tanker truck is helpful if we are not near a fire hydrant.

Fire trucks also carry axes, crowbars, and other things we need to do our jobs.

When I'm on duty, I live upstairs, above the fire trucks. There we have a room full of beds for sleeping. We fix our meals and eat together in the fire station kitchen. We have a bathroom and a room where we can read, watch television, or talk on the phone. We also have an exercise room because we must stay physically fit.

We have a dog at the fire station. His name is Flash. He is a Dalmatian.

Fire departments started keeping Dalmatians a long time ago, when fire engines were pulled by horses. Dalmatians weren't afraid of horses. On the way to a fire, Dalmatians ran out in front of the engines to clear the streets.

When we are fighting fires, we wear special coats, pants, boots, helmets, and gloves. These special clothes protect us from the fire.

Fires create lots of smoke, so firefighters also wear face masks and air tanks to help us breathe. We go to special training schools every year to help us stay good at our jobs.

When there is a fire, the alarm sounds at the fire station. The firefighters spring to action.

We put on our special coats, pants, boots, helmets, and gloves very quickly. We have to be ready to leave the fire station within a few minutes. Instead of using the stairs, we slide down a pole so we can get to our fire trucks in a hurry.

Between emergencies, we make sure the fire engines and equipment are in good shape. The alarm is ringing! I'm glad we checked the trucks. We have to go fight a fire now!